Arctic
Whale Danger!

Rob Waring, *Series Editor*

HEINLE
CENGAGE Learning™

Australia • Brazil • Japan • Korea • Mexico • Singapore • Spain • United Kingdom • United States

Words to Know

This story is set in the Arctic **Ocean**.

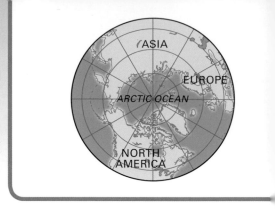

A **The Arctic Shore.** Write each word in the picture next to the correct definition.

1. the land next to the ocean: _____.
2. a large white sea animal: _____.
3. hard pieces of water formed in the cold: _____.
4. big stones that you find sometimes find near the sea: _____.
5. a part of the sea that is nearly closed in by land: _____.
6. a large sea animal that has a long object on its head: _____.

The Arctic Shore

B Arctic Animals. Look at the pictures and captions. Complete the paragraph with the correct form of the **bolded** words.

Narwhals have a long tusk.

An **adult beluga whale** and her **calf**.

Codfish swimming in the ocean.

Many kinds of whales live in the Arctic Ocean. 1)_____ are very big and white. 2)_____ have a long tusk. A baby whale is called a 3)_____. Most whales like to eat fish. One kind of fish they eat is called 4)_____.

Beluga whales are very social animals. This means that they like to be around other whales. Their relationships with the whales around them are very strong. A mother and her calf will often swim together for three years. Beluga whale calves are gray when they are born. They turn white, like the ice around them, when they become adults.

It may seem like the beluga whales have a very happy life, but sometimes this isn't the case...

CD 1, Track 1

On one particular day, a group of beluga whales is swimming in the bay. When the **tide**[1] goes out, the adult belugas are able to swim back to deeper water.

However, one young beluga has gone too far onto the shore. It can't get back to the water. Suddenly, play time becomes a **race against time!**[2]

[1]**tide:** the regular rising and falling of the ocean
[2]**race against time:** need to hurry or act quickly

The Sun now becomes the whale's biggest danger. It's very hot on the young beluga's body. The whale could easily **sunburn**[3], get too hot, and die. The young beluga has nothing to cover it. It's totally helpless. The other belugas can only watch and wait as the calf tries to move.

As the beluga calf moves around on the shore, the rocks cut its skin. More and more time passes. The minutes slowly turn into hours. There's nothing that the whale can do for now. It can only wait for the tide to come back.

Everyone has **made a mistake**[4] in their life. However, this mistake could be deadly for the little beluga. Finally, the tide starts coming back. But will it be soon enough to help the baby beluga?

---

[3]**sunburn:** when the skin becomes red and hot from the sun
[4]**make a mistake:** do something wrong

Predict

Answer the questions. Then, scan page 11 to check your answers.

1. What will happen to the beluga calf?

2. Why do you think that?

Slowly the sea starts to come back onto the shore. The water brings the very tired beluga back to life. It begins to move. Then, it begins to push… and push…and push. With one last energetic push, the beluga is **free**[5]! At last, it's able to return to the sea.

The young beluga quickly joins the other whales in the deep water once again. The young calf is fine. Perhaps it has learned something from this bad experience. Perhaps it will be more careful the next time it's near the shore!

---

[5]**free:** able to go where it wants

Young belugas are not the only arctic whales that can get in trouble. The narwhal is another type of whale that lives in the Arctic Ocean. They are a very unusual kind of whale. They have a tusk, or horn, that can grow as long as **nine feet**![6] The tusk is actually a kind of tooth that grows through the narwhal's top **lip**.[7] Before, no one knew why the narwhals had this tusk. Most people thought that the whales only used it to fight other whales. However, scientists now think that the tusk helps narwhals sense environmental conditions, like **temperature**.[8]

[6]**nine feet:** 2.74 meters
[7]**lip:** the area around the mouth
[8]**temperature:** how hot or cold something is

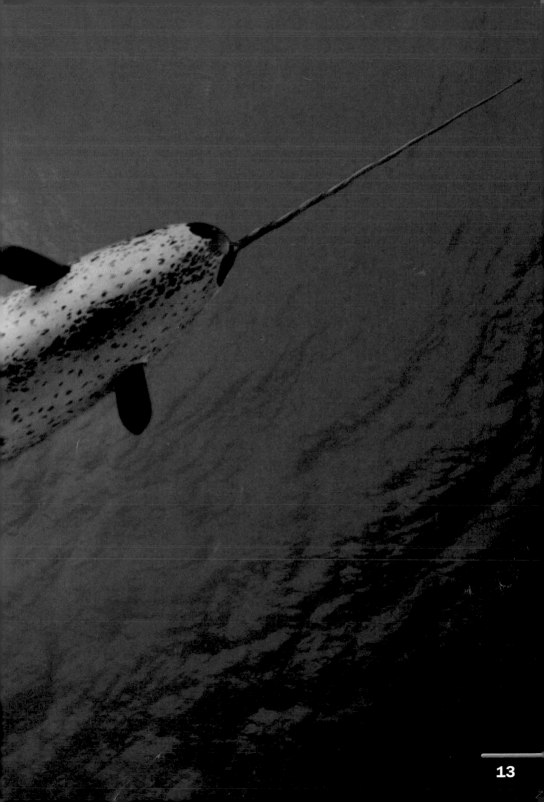

Narwhals usually swim in small groups. However, on this day the number of narwhals swimming together is much larger. The exact number may vary, but sometimes the group might grow to more than a hundred whales! The whales are swimming together as they look for a favorite food—codfish.

After a while, the narwhals follow a group of codfish into the bay. But they're taking a big risk. The bay has ice all around it. If the ice moves and closes the opening to the bay, the whales could become **trapped**.[9]

---

[9]**trapped:** unable to move

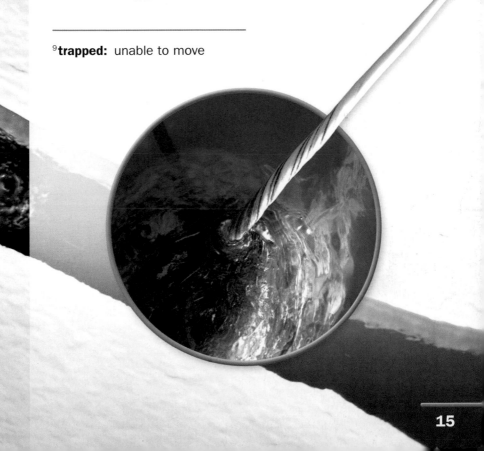

And that's exactly what happens! Suddenly, the ice moves in and closes off the way out to the open sea. The narwhals can't get out of the bay. They're trapped! Not even their long tusks can help them now…

All the narwhals now have to swim in a very small area of water that has no ice on it. It's a very difficult situation for the narwhals. Whales **breathe oxygen.**[10] If the ice moves closer and covers the water, the narwhals can't come out of the water. They won't be able to get air! They'll have to swim out from under the ice to find it or they'll die. Will the whales be able to find air in time?

---

[10]**breathe oxygen:** use air in their bodies

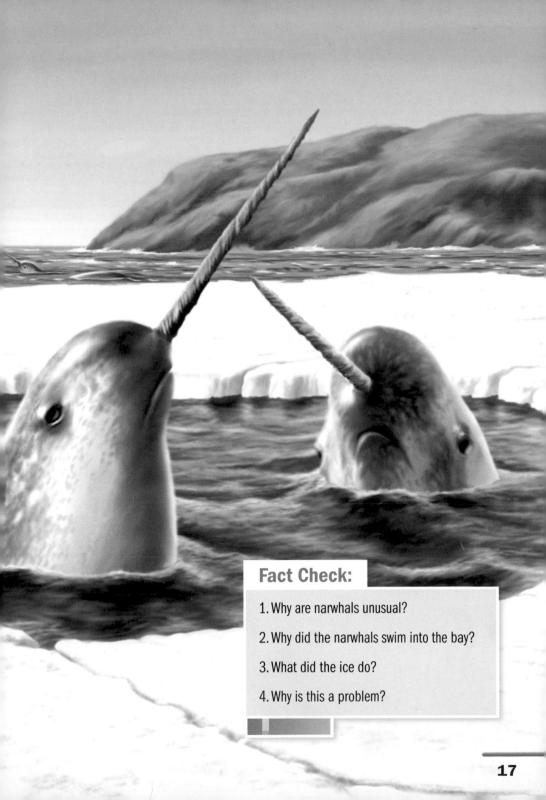

Fact Check:

1. Why are narwhals unusual?

2. Why did the narwhals swim into the bay?

3. What did the ice do?

4. Why is this a problem?

Suddenly, the ice moves. The way out of the
bay and into the ocean is open again. Finally, the
narwhals are not trapped anymore. They are free.
They're free to look for fish. Free to swim the seas.
Free to do whatever they want to do—with that
very unusual tusk!

After You Read

1. The beluga whale is _____ very social animal.
   A. the
   B. an
   C. that
   D. a

2. What color is an adult beluga whale?
   A. gray-white
   B. gray
   C. white
   D. none of the above

3. On page 7, 'it' refers to:
   A. the shore
   B. a baby beluga
   C. the tide
   D. deeper water

4. What is a good heading for page 8?
   A. Young Whale in Trouble
   B. The Tide Comes Back
   C. Adult Beluga Makes Deadly Mistake
   D. Whale Finds New Home

5. After the tide comes back, where does the young whale go?
   A. to the rocks
   B. to the other whales
   C. to the shore
   D. to the ice

6. What is one known way the narwhals use their tusks?
   A. to fight other whales
   B. to swim better
   C. to get codfish
   D. no one knows

7. What's a good heading for page 12?
    A. Looking for Codfish
    B. Ice Moves in Suddenly
    C. The Arctic Ocean
    D. An Unusual, Whale

8. On page 15, 'taking a big risk' can be replaced by:
    A. being difficult
    B. very unusual
    C. possibly in danger
    D. looking for fish

9. The narwhals become trapped in the _____.
    A. shore
    B. ocean
    C. open sea
    D. bay

10. How do the narwhals get free?
    A. The tide comes in.
    B. The ice opens a way.
    C. They swim under the ice.
    D. The ice moves closer.

11. Which is NOT true for both narwhals and belugas in this story?
    A. They breathe oxygen.
    B. They like to swim with others.
    C. They live in the Arctic Ocean.
    D. They have tusks.

Visiting
the Arctic

You've seen pictures of beluga whales and narwhals. You've read something about how they live in the Arctic Ocean. But have you ever thought about visiting the Arctic yourself? Every year thousands of people do. They get there on ships that leave from cities in Canada, Russia, and parts of Europe. Here are some questions that people planning a trip to the Arctic often ask.

Tourists on a ship in the Arctic Ocean

Q: WHAT KINDS OF SHIPS GO TO THE ARCTIC?

A: Only special ships can go to the Arctic. They must be very strong because of all the ice in the Arctic Ocean. Many of the ships are also quite small. The largest ones hold no more than 100 people. Most of them hold around 50 people. Some ships leave from small towns in northern Canada. Tourists usually have to fly there from Montreal. People can also leave from cities in northern Europe or the northern part of Russia.

Q: WHEN IS THE BEST TIME TO GO?

A: The best time to visit the Arctic Ocean is during the months of July, and August. During these months, the temperatures are usually above 45 degrees Fahrenheit during the day. In January and February, the temperature can be very cold. During these months, ice covers many parts of the Arctic Ocean and ships cannot pass through. In some places this ice can be several feet thick.

> **"Most travelers say that their trip to the Arctic was very interesting."**

Q: WHAT DO PEOPLE DO ON THE SHIP?

A: Most ships offer classes every day. People can learn about the things they will see on shore. They can also learn about the history of the area. Who first found the area? What did they see there? There are also often classes about local sea animals, like birds, whales, or codfish. All of these animals are common in the Arctic. Most travelers say that their trip to the Arctic was very interesting. Some think it's the best vacation they've ever taken.

CD 1, Track 2

Word Count: 312
Time: _____

Vocabulary List

adult (3, 4, 7)
bay (2, 15, 16, 17, 18)
beluga whale (2, 3, 4, 7, 8, 11, 12)
breathe oxygen (16)
calf (3, 4, 8, 11)
codfish (3, 15)
free (11, 18)
ice (2, 15, 16, 18)
lip (12)
make (a) mistake (8)
narwhal (2, 3, 12, 15, 16, 18)
ocean (2, 3, 18)
race against time (7)
rocks (2, 8)
shore (2, 11)
sunburn (8)
swim (3, 7, 15, 16)
temperature (12)
tide (7, 8)
trapped (15, 16, 18)